DON LIVINGSTON

Guide for First-Time Dog Owners

How to Raise a Healthy and Happy Puppy

First edition

This book was professionally typeset on Reedsy.
Find out more at reedsy.com

Dedicated to the dogs who have brought me joy, past and present:

Season

Napoleon

Pieface

Tiny

Mandy

Sheba

C.J.

Cindy

Ginger

James

Woody

Porthos

George

Lucy

Ollie

Oden

Marshal

Copper

Contents

1 Introduction 1

2 Are You Ready for Dog Ownership? 3

3 Finding the Right Dog 5

4 Preparing Your Home and Yard 9

5 Essential Supplies for Your Dog 12

6 Veterinary Care and Medical Information 15

7 Training and Socialization Tips 19

8 Nutrition and Exercise 23

9 Traveling with Your Dog 26

10 When Your Dog Can't Travel with You 29

11 End-of-Life Considerations 33

12 Conclusion 36

13 References 38

About the Author 40

1

Introduction

Welcome to "Guide for First-Time Dog Owners: How to Raise a Healthy and Happy Pet". Whether you're a single individual, a young couple, or a budding family, embarking on the journey of dog ownership can be an exciting and rewarding experience. This book is crafted specifically for those who are venturing into the world of dog companionship for the first time, providing you with the knowledge and tools you need to become confident and responsible pet parents.

Owning a dog comes with its unique set of challenges, joys, and responsibilities. From the moment you welcome a furry friend into your home, expect to be met with boundless love, unwavering loyalty, and countless moments of pure joy. Yet, alongside these heartwarming moments, there are also practical considerations and responsibilities to be mindful of. From training and socialization to veterinary care and nutrition, there's much to learn and navigate.

However, fear not! While the journey of dog ownership may seem daunting at first, it's also incredibly rewarding. Through this book, we aim to equip you with the knowledge, guidance, and support you need to thrive as a first-time dog owner. From understanding whether you're ready for the commitment to finding the perfect companion puppy for your lifestyle, each chapter is designed to empower you with practical advice and insights.

So, if you're ready to begin this wonderful journey, then let's dive in. By the end of this book, you'll feel confident and prepared to provide your new four-legged friend with a life filled with health, happiness, and endless tail wags. Get ready to unleash the joy of dog ownership and create lasting memories that will warm your heart for years to come.

2

Are You Ready for Dog Ownership?

Before you take the leap into dog ownership, it's vital to assess your readiness for the commitment ahead. Owning a dog entails more than just cuddles and playtime; it requires dedication, time, and financial resources. Let's explore the key factors to consider before bringing a pet into your life.

Signs of Readiness:

Assess your lifestyle and daily routine. Can you accommodate the needs of a dog, including feeding, exercise, and socialization? Dogs require consistent care and attention, so it's crucial to ensure that you have the time to dedicate to your new companion.

Understanding the Commitment:

Owning a dog is a long-term commitment. From daily walks to emergency vet visits, you must be prepared to give priority to your dog's well-being. This commitment extends for the entirety of your dog's life, which can be up to a decade or more.

Assessing Your Lifestyle:

Consider how a dog will fit into your current lifestyle. Are you an active individual who enjoys outdoor activities, or do you prefer a more relaxed pace of life? Understanding your lifestyle will help you choose a dog breed and temperament that aligns with your preferences.

Financial Considerations:

Owning a dog can be a significant financial investment. Initial costs, including adoption fees or purchase prices, can range from $50 to $2000 or more depending on the source and breed. Additionally, ongoing expenses such as food, grooming, veterinary care, and supplies can amount to $1000 or more per year. It's essential to evaluate your financial situation and ensure that you can afford to provide for your dog's needs without compromising your own financial stability.

So you can see that assessing your readiness for dog ownership involves considering various factors, including your lifestyle, time availability, and financial resources. By taking the time to evaluate these aspects, you can ensure that you're prepared to welcome a furry friend into your home and provide it with the love, care, and attention it deserves. Being sure of these factors is only fair to both of you; because from now on, you will be a team.

3

Finding the Right Dog

Selecting the perfect canine companion is a significant decision that requires careful consideration. Your new friend will become an integral part of your life, so it's essential to choose a dog that aligns with your lifestyle, preferences, and values. In this chapter, we'll explore various avenues for finding the right dog, including researching breeds, exploring adoption options, and understanding the importance of ethical breeding practices.

Researching Breeds and Considerations:

With hundreds of dog breeds to choose from, it's essential to research and understand their characteristics, temperaments, and needs. Consider factors such as size, energy level, grooming requirements, and compatibility with children or other pets. Reputable sources such as the American Kennel Club (AKC) and breed-specific associations provide valuable insights into breed standards and traits. Additionally, don't overlook the option of mixed-breed dogs, which often possess a unique blend of qualities from multiple breeds. You might find it helpful to watch YouTube videos that feature a variety of breeds to determine which ones appeal to you the most. What owners reveal about their dog's temperament, habits, or health concerns in these videos can sometimes sway you one way or the other.

Understanding Shelter Adoption:

Shelters and rescue organizations offer a diverse selection of dogs, including mixed breeds and purebreds. Adopting from a shelter not only gives a deserving dog a second chance at a loving home, but also helps combat pet overpopulation. Shelters typically assess each dog's temperament and behavior to match them with suitable families. Additionally, many shelters provide veterinary care, vaccinations, and spaying/neutering services before adoption, which will save you the expense of having it done later. By adopting from a shelter, you're not only saving a life, but also enriching your own.

Beware of Disreputable Breeders:

Unfortunately, not all breeders focus on the well-being of their dogs. Some unethical breeders prioritize profit over the health and welfare of their animals, engaging in practices such as over breeding, inadequate care, and poor living conditions. These breeders often operate without proper licenses or certifications and may sell puppies through online advertisements or pet stores (but keep in mind that reputable breeders may also advertise, so this is not a blanket indictment on all such activities). However, it is crucial to research breeders thoroughly, visit their facilities in person, and ask for references from previous customers. Ethical breeders prioritize the health, temperament, and genetic diversity of their dogs and are transparent about their breeding practices.

Choosing Ethical Breeding Practices:

When purchasing a dog from a breeder, look for those who demonstrate a commitment to ethical breeding practices. Ethical breeders conduct health screenings on breeding stock, provide proper socialization for puppies, and offer lifetime support to puppy buyers. They welcome questions, encourage visits to their facilities, and provide documentation of health clearances and pedigrees. By supporting ethical breeders, you're contributing to the betterment of the breed and ensuring that your new dog comes from a reputable source.

Finding the right dog involves careful research, consideration, and thoughtful decision-making. Whether you choose to adopt from a shelter or purchase from a breeder, prioritize the well-being and happiness of your future companion. By understanding the traits and needs of different breeds, exploring adoption options, and supporting ethical breeding practices, you will be on your way to finding the perfect companion to share your life's adventures. So, search with an open heart and a commitment to providing a loving and nurturing home for your new best friend.

4

Preparing Your Home and Yard

As you eagerly anticipate the arrival of your new canine companion, it's crucial to ensure that your home and yard are safe and welcoming environments. Let's discuss the essential steps to prepare your living space for your dog or puppy, including identifying potential hazards, securing your yard, and investing in necessary equipment. Additionally, we'll explore online resources to help you navigate the world of pet safety and provide valuable information on substances, foods, chemicals, and vegetation that may be harmful to dogs.

Creating a Safe Environment:

Before bringing your new dog home, take a proactive approach to identify and eliminate potential hazards. Remove or securely store household items that could pose a danger, such as electrical cords, toxic cleaning products, antifreeze, and medications. Keep in mind, if you live in a cold climate, certain snow and ice melt products can be harmful to dogs' paws. Also, foods like chocolate, grapes, onions, and xylitol can be toxic to dogs if ingested, so it's essential to keep them out of reach. Utilize baby gates to block off areas that are off-limits to your dog, and consider using pet-friendly deterrents to discourage unwanted behaviors.

Puppy-Proofing Tips:

If you're welcoming a playful puppy into your home, take extra precautions to puppy-proof your space. Puppies are naturally curious and prone to exploring with their mouths, so be sure to remove small objects, choking hazards, and potential toxins. Secure trash cans with lids, use cord protectors to cover electrical cords, and avoid leaving shoes, socks, or other tempting items within your puppy's reach, until it is clear that they have outgrown any destructive chewing habit. Provide plenty of safe chew toys and supervise your puppy closely to prevent accidents and promote positive chewing behavior.

Choosing Appropriate Spaces:

Designate specific areas of your home and yard for your dog's use, including sleeping, eating, and play areas. Create a comfortable sleeping area with a cozy bed or crate in a quiet, draft-free location. Outdoors, ensure that your yard is securely fenced to prevent escapes and keep your dog safe from potential dangers like traffic or wildlife. Consider using GPS collars or underground fence boundaries to provide additional containment for your dog and peace of mind for you.

Necessary Equipment Installation:

Invest in essential equipment to meet your dog's needs and enhance their safety and comfort. This includes sturdy food and water bowls, a leash and collar or harness for walks, and identification tags with your contact information. Consider installing a pet first-aid kit to handle minor injuries or emergencies, and stock up on grooming supplies like brushes, nail clippers, and shampoo.

Online Resources for Pet Safety:

Take advantage of online resources to educate yourself about substances, foods, chemicals, and vegetation that may be harmful to dogs. If you want to know more, be sure to investigate websites such as the American Society for the Prevention of Cruelty to Animals (ASPCA) Poison Control Center (www.aspca.org/pet-care/animal-poison-control). They provide comprehensive lists of toxic substances and guidance on what to do if your dog ingests something harmful. Additionally, consult recognized sources such as veterinary websites, pet care blogs, and breed-specific forums for valuable insights and advice on keeping your dog safe and healthy.

Preparing your home and yard for the arrival of your new dog is a crucial step in ensuring their safety, comfort, and well-being. By taking proactive measures to identify and eliminate potential hazards, securing your living space, and investing in necessary equipment, you'll create a safe and welcoming environment where your dog can thrive. With careful preparation and attention to detail, you'll set the stage for a lifetime of love, happiness, and companionship with your new best friend.

5

Essential Supplies for Your Dog

Preparing your home for your canine buddy involves gathering essential supplies to meet their needs and ensure their comfort and well-being. We will now discuss the must-have items you'll need to welcome your dog into your home, from basic necessities to optional accessories.

Making a Shopping List:

Before bringing your dog home, it's essential to make a comprehensive shopping list of necessary supplies. Start with the basics, including food and water bowls, a comfortable bed or crate, a leash and collar or harness, and identification tags with your contact information. Consider your dog's size, breed, and age when selecting these items to ensure they are appropriate and comfortable.

Basic Supplies:

In addition to the essentials mentioned above, there are several other basic supplies you'll need to care for your dog. These include high-quality dog food appropriate for your dog's age and size, grooming supplies such as brushes, nail clippers, and shampoo, and cleaning supplies for accidents and messes. Look for reputable brands recommended by veterinarians and dog experts, such as Royal Canin, Hill's Science Diet, and Purina Pro Plan.

Must-Have Items:

- Food and water bowls
- Comfortable bed or crate
- Leash and collar or harness
- Identification tags with your contact information
- High-quality dog food appropriate for your dog's age and size
- Grooming supplies (brushes, nail clippers, shampoo)
- Cleaning supplies for accidents and messes

Desirable Items (Optional):

- Interactive puzzle toys
- Durable chew toys
- Squeaky plush toys
- Treat-dispensing toys
- Doggy toothbrush and toothpaste
- Training treats

- Doggy backpack or harness for outings
- Pet first-aid kit
- Elevated food and water bowls for larger breeds

Gathering essential supplies for your new dog is an exciting step in preparing for their arrival. A shopping list of high-quality products recommended by experts, can help ensure that your dog has everything it needs to feel accepted and loved in its new home.

6

Veterinary Care and Medical Information

As a responsible dog owner, providing proper veterinary care for your new dog is essential to ensure their health and well-being. We now turn our attention to the importance of regular veterinary check-ups, vaccinations, preventive care, and common medical procedures. Additionally, we'll explore the options for pet health insurance plans, potential costs, types of coverage, and websites where you can learn if insurance is a viable option for you and your dog.

Importance of Veterinary Care:

Regular veterinary check-ups are crucial for maintaining your dog's health and detecting any potential issues early on. During these visits, your veterinarian will perform a thorough physical examination, administer necessary vaccinations, and discuss preventive care measures such as parasite control and dental health. Veterinary care also provides an opportunity to address any questions or concerns you may have about your dog's health and behavior. Vets are trained to know about the most common problems of particular breeds, and can be preemptive in their care and treatment.

Vaccinations:

Vaccinations help to protect dogs against potentially life-threatening diseases. Common vaccinations for dogs include rabies, distemper, parvovirus, adenovirus, and parainfluenza. The cost of vaccinations can vary depending on factors such as your location, the veterinarian's fees, and the specific vaccines required. On average, expect to pay between $75 to $100 for a basic set of core vaccinations for your dog.

Preventive Care:

In addition to vaccinations, preventive care measures such as flea and tick prevention, heartworm prevention, and regular dental care are essential for maintaining your dog's health. Flea and tick preventives could cost between $20 to $60 per month, while heartworm preventives range from $5 to $15 per month, depending on the size of your dog and the type of medication. Regular dental cleanings may cost between $200 to $600, depending on the extent of dental disease and any additional procedures required.

Common Medical Procedures:

While preventive care measures can help reduce the risk of illness and disease, dogs may still require medical procedures at some points in their lives. Common medical procedures for dogs include spaying or neutering, dental extractions, ear cleanings, and treatment for injuries or illnesses. The cost of these procedures can vary widely depending on factors such as your location, the veterinarian's fees, and the specific needs of your dog. On average, spaying or neutering may cost between $200 to $500, while dental extractions can range from $300 to $800 or more. It may be wise to consult veterinarian clinics in your area so you won't be surprised later on.

Pet Health Insurance Plans:

Pet health insurance plans provide coverage for veterinary expenses, including routine care, emergencies, and unexpected illnesses or injuries. These plans typically offer various levels of coverage, including accident-only plans, basic plans covering accidents and illnesses, and comprehensive plans that include preventive care and wellness services.

Websites such as Pet Insurance Review (www.petinsurancereview.com) and Healthy Paws Pet Insurance (www.healthypawspetinsurance.com) offer comprehensive information on different types of pet insurance plans, coverage options, and customer reviews to help you choose the best plan for your dog. Your veterinarian will also be able to assist you in making decisions that are best for you and your pet.

Types of Coverage:

Pet health insurance plans may cover a range of veterinary expenses, including:

- Ilnesses and injuries
- Diagnostic tests and treatments
- Prescription medications
- Surgery and hospitalization
- Emergency and specialty care
- Preventive care and wellness services (optional)

By scheduling regular check-ups, staying up-to-date on vaccinations, and providing preventive care measures, you can help keep your companion happy and healthy for years to come. Consider exploring pet health insurance options to help offset the costs of veterinary care and provide financial protection in the event of unexpected expenses. Remember, investing in your dog's health and well-being is an important part of responsible pet ownership, and the peace of mind knowing your dog is covered in case of illness or injury is invaluable.

7

Training and Socialization Tips

Training and socialization can help your new dog become a well-behaved and well-adjusted member of your family and community. In this chapter, we'll provide tips for getting started, and recommend resources for further research to help you navigate the training process with confidence.

Importance of Training:

T raining is not just about teaching your dog basic commands; it's also about establishing clear communication, building trust and rapport, and fostering a positive relationship between you and your dog. Training helps your dog understand what is expected, prevents unwanted behaviors, and strengthens the bond between dog and owner. Whether you're teaching basic obedience commands like sit, stay, and come, or addressing behavioral issues like jumping, barking, or leash pulling, consistent training is the key to success.

Socialization:

Socialization is equally important for your dog's overall well-being and behavior. Gradually exposing your dog to a variety of people, animals, environments, and experiences helps them develop confidence, resilience, and good manners. Proper socialization can prevent fear, anxiety, and aggression, making your dog more adaptable and better able to navigate the world around them. Start socializing your dog from a young age and continue exposing them to new experiences throughout their life in a controlled and thoughtful manner.

Getting Started with Training:

Begin training your dog as soon as you bring them home, using positive reinforcement techniques such as praise, treats, toys, and affection to motivate and reward desired behaviors. Keep training sessions short, fun, and engaging, and be patient and consistent in your approach. Focus on teaching one command or behavior at a time, gradually increasing difficulty as your dog progresses. Consider enrolling in a basic obedience class or working with a professional dog trainer for personalized guidance and support.

Resources for Research:

As you embark on your training journey with your new dog, there are numerous resources available to help you learn and grow together. Websites such as the American Kennel Club (www.akc.org), the Association of Professional Dog Trainers (www.apdt.com), and the Karen Pryor Academy (www.clickertraining.com) offer valuable information, articles, videos, and online courses on various aspects of dog training and behavior. Additionally, books by renowned dog trainers and behaviorists, such as Patricia McConnell, Ian Dunbar, and Karen Pryor, provide in-depth insights and practical tips for effective training and socialization.

Training and socialization are essential for helping your new dog become a well-behaved and well-adjusted member of your family. By establishing clear communication, building trust and rapport, and providing positive reinforcement, you can teach your dog basic obedience commands and address behavioral issues with patience and consistency. Remember to start socializing your dog from a young age and continue exposing them to new experiences throughout their life. With dedication and perseverance, you'll set the stage for a lifetime of happiness, harmony, and mutual understanding with your canine companion

8

Nutrition and Exercise

We now delve into the importance of a balanced diet and a regular exercise regimen for your dog. It will be of benefit to you and your pet to be aware of the research and resources available to help you make informed decisions about your dog's diet and fitness routine.

Importance of Nutrition:

Nutrition plays a pivotal role in your dog's health, providing the essential nutrients they need for growth, energy, and vitality. A balanced diet tailored to your dog's age, size, breed, and activity level supports healthy development, maintains optimal weight and body condition, and strengthens the immune system. Choosing high-quality, nutritious food is crucial for promoting your dog's well-being and longevity.

Selecting the Right Diet:

When selecting a diet for your dog, consider factors such as their age, size, breed, activity level, and any specific dietary needs or preferences. Opt for high-quality commercial dog food that meets the nutritional standards set by reputable organizations such as the Association of American Feed Control Officials (AAFCO) for complete and balanced nutrition. Look for brands that use wholesome, natural ingredients and avoid artificial additives, fillers, and by-products.

Common Health Concerns:

Proper nutrition can help prevent and manage a variety of health issues in dogs, including obesity, digestive disorders, allergies, and joint problems. Be mindful of your dog's calorie intake and portion sizes to prevent weight gain and obesity-related health issues. Monitor their body condition regularly and consult your veterinarian if you notice any signs of dietary sensitivities or health concerns. Additionally, provide plenty of fresh water at all times to support hydration and kidney function.

Importance of Exercise:

Regular exercise is essential for keeping your dog physically and mentally fit, preventing obesity, promoting cardiovascular health, and reducing the risk of behavioral problems. Aim for a minimum of 30 minutes to an hour of moderate exercise each day, tailored to your dog's age, breed, size, and energy level. Activities such as walking, running, hiking, swimming, and interactive play sessions provide opportunities for physical activity and mental stimulation. Many dog owners have discovered that an added bonus to their dog's exercise routine is that it also becomes the owner's exercise routine as well, which contributes to the health of both.

Resources for Further Research:

As you navigate the world of dog nutrition and exercise, there are numerous resources available to help you make informed decisions and provide the best possible care for your furry friend. Websites such as the American Kennel Club (www.akc.org), the American College of Veterinary Nutrition (www.acvn.org), and the Association for Pet Obesity Prevention (www.petobesityprevention.org) offer valuable information, articles, and resources on topics ranging from pet nutrition and dietary guidelines to exercise recommendations and weight management tips.

Proper nutrition and exercise are fundamental aspects of ensuring the health of your new dog. By selecting a balanced diet tailored to your dog's individual needs and establishing a regular exercise routine, you can help them live a long, happy, and healthy life. Utilize resources such as veterinary organizations, pet nutrition associations, and respected websites to enhance your knowledge and make informed decisions about your dog's diet and fitness regimen. With dedication and care, you'll provide your companion with the best possible foundation for a lifetime of health and happiness.

9

Traveling with Your Dog

Traveling with your dog can be a rewarding experience, whether you're embarking on a road trip, going camping, or visiting family and friends. Many dogs enjoy accompanying their owners on short errands, which allows them to evaluate the effects of motion on their dogs and determine whether car sickness might be an issue. Now, let's explore tips and considerations for traveling safely and comfortably with your furry companion, including car travel, rest stops, essential items to take along, pet-friendly accommodations, and places where pets may not be allowed.

Car Travel Tips:

Before hitting the road with your dog, it's essential to prepare for a safe and enjoyable journey. Secure your dog in a well-ventilated crate, carrier, or harness to prevent them from roaming freely in the car and causing distractions. Ensure your dog is wearing a collar with identification tags and is up-to-date on vaccinations. It might also be a good safeguard to check with your veterinarian about adding a microchip to your dog in case it becomes lost during the trip. Plan regular rest stops every 2-3 hours to allow your dog to stretch its legs, use the bathroom, and stay hydrated.

Rest Stop Considerations:

When stopping at rest areas or roadside parks, always keep your dog on a leash and clean up after them to be considerate of other travelers. Look for designated pet areas with grassy areas or pet waste stations for convenience. Bring along a collapsible water bowl and plenty of fresh water to keep your dog hydrated during the journey. Avoid leaving your dog unattended in the car, especially in hot weather, as temperatures can quickly rise to dangerous levels.

Essential Items to Take Along:

When traveling with your dog, be sure to pack essential items to ensure their comfort and well-being. These may include:

- Food and water bowls
- Ample supply of food and treats
- Leash, collar, and identification tags
- Waste bags for clean-up
- Travel crate or carrier
- Comfort items such as blankets or toys
- Medications and first-aid kit
- Grooming supplies (brush, nail clippers, etc.)
- Travel documents (vaccination records, health certificates, etc.)

Pet-Friendly Accommodations:

When planning overnight stays during your trip, look for pet-friendly accommodations that welcome dogs. Many hotels, motels, and vacation rentals offer pet-friendly rooms or facilities for an additional fee. Be sure to call ahead and confirm pet policies, restrictions, and any additional charges before making reservations. Websites such as BringFido (www.bringfido.com) and Airbnb (www.airbnb.com) offer search filters for pet-friendly accommodations to make planning your trip easier.

Places Where Pets Are Usually Not Allowed:

While many public places and attractions welcome dogs, there are some areas where pets may not be permitted. These may include restaurants, grocery stores, museums, galleries, and certain outdoor recreational areas such as national parks or wildlife reserves. Be mindful of posted signs and regulations indicating where pets are not allowed and respect the rules to avoid any potential issues or fines. If in doubt, check websites, or call ahead. Don't leave it to chance.

Traveling with your dog can be a wonderful opportunity to create lasting memories and share new adventures together. Whether you're exploring new destinations or visiting familiar places, traveling with your dog allows you to experience the world from a unique perspective and strengthen the bond you share. Safe travels!

10

When Your Dog Can't Travel with You

There may be times when you need to leave your dog behind while you travel, whether it's for a short trip or an extended period. In this chapter, we'll explore tips and considerations for ensuring your dog's well-being and comfort when they can't travel with you, including kenneling your dog briefly or arranging for care with neighbors, friends, or relatives. We'll discuss planning ahead, avoiding potential problems, prepping your dog for a new environment, educating temporary caregivers, and ensuring a temporary kennel is reputable.

Kenneling Your Dog

If you need to leave your dog in a kennel or boarding facility for a brief period, it's essential to choose a reputable and trustworthy establishment. Research local kennels and read reviews from other pet owners to ensure they provide quality care and a safe environment for your dog. Visit the facility beforehand to tour the facilities, meet the staff, and ask questions about their services, policies, and procedures. Provide detailed instructions about your dog's feeding schedule, medication needs, exercise routine, and any special requirements to ensure it receives the best possible care during its stay. If possible, see if you may leave your dog's crate to provide it with a familiar and secure retreat during its stay.

Arranging Care with Neighbors, Friends, or Relatives:

If you prefer to leave your dog with neighbors, friends, or relatives while you travel, it's crucial to choose caregivers who are responsible, reliable, willing, and capable of caring for your dog. Schedule a meeting to discuss your dog's needs, routines, and preferences with potential caregivers and ensure they have access to your dog's food, supplies, and veterinary information. Provide written instructions detailing your dog's care needs, emergency contact information, and any relevant medical history. Consider arranging a trial stay or playdate beforehand to familiarize your dog with the caregivers and their home environment.

Planning Ahead and Avoiding Potential Problems:

Whether you're kenneling your dog or arranging for care with temporary caregivers, you will find that it is important to plan ahead and address any potential problems or concerns before you leave your pet. Ensure your dog is up-to-date on vaccinations, flea and tick prevention, and any necessary medications before its stay. Pack an overnight bag with your dog's essentials, including food, treats, medications, toys, bedding, and comfort items to help them feel at ease in their new environment. Provide contact information for your veterinarian and instructions for contacting you in case of emergencies or concerns. Consider checking in by phone, or even a video call, to see how things are going while you are away.

Prepping Your Dog for a New Environment:

Transitioning to a new environment can be stressful for dogs, so it's essential to prepare them as much as possible for their temporary stay. Take your dog for a visit to the kennel or caregiver's home beforehand to familiarize it with the surroundings and introduce it to the caregivers. Bring along familiar items such as its bed, toys, and blankets to provide comfort and security during their stay. Maintain a positive attitude and reassure your dog that it will be well cared for while you're away.

Educating Temporary Caregivers:

Before you leave, take the time to educate temporary caregivers about your dog's habits, preferences, and personality traits to ensure they can provide appropriate care and attention. Provide detailed instructions for feeding, exercise, grooming, and any specific behavioral cues or commands your dog responds to. Encourage caregivers to spend quality time with your dog, engage in interactive play, and provide plenty of love and affection to help alleviate any stress or anxiety during your absence. Be sure to inform them of both acceptable and unacceptable disciplinary measures so the dog has continuity of care and is not confused by unfamiliar procedures.

Ensuring a Brief-Stay Kennel is Reputable:

If you opt to kennel your dog for a brief period, it's crucial to choose a reputable facility that prioritizes your dog's safety, well-being, and comfort. Research local kennels and boarding facilities to ensure they are licensed, bonded, and accredited by respected organizations such as the American Kennel Club (AKC) or the Pet Care Services Association (PCSA). Visit the facility in person to assess cleanliness, security, and overall conditions, and ask for references from other pet owners who have used their services.

Leaving your dog behind when you travel can be a difficult decision, but with proper planning and preparation, you can ensure it receives the best possible care and attention in your absence. Whether you choose to kennel your dog briefly or arrange for care with neighbors, friends, or relatives, try to prioritize its safety, well-being, and comfort. By planning ahead, you can enjoy peace of mind knowing your furry companion is in good hands while you're away.

11

End-of-Life Considerations

This topic is rarely considered when folks embark upon the journey of pet companionship, but a bit of awareness at the start can be beneficial down the road. As much as we wish our furry friends could stay by our side forever, the reality is that their time with us is finite. In this chapter, we'll explore the sensitive topic of end-of-life considerations for your beloved canine companion, including how to recognize signs of declining health, making decisions about palliative care and euthanasia, and coping with grief and loss.

Recognizing Signs of Declining Health:

As your dog ages, you may notice changes in their behavior, appetite, mobility, and overall demeanor. These changes can be indicative of underlying health issues such as arthritis, organ dysfunction, or cancer. Pay close attention to subtle changes in your dog's habits and seek veterinary advice if you notice any concerning symptoms, such as loss of appetite, lethargy, difficulty breathing, or changes in bathroom habits. Regular veterinary check-ups can help monitor your dog's health and detect any potential issues early on.

Palliative Care Options:

If your dog is diagnosed with a terminal illness or experiences a decline in health due to old age, you may consider palliative care to keep them comfortable and improve their quality of life. Palliative care focuses on managing pain, alleviating discomfort, and providing supportive care to enhance your dog's well-being during their final days or weeks. Your veterinarian can work with you to develop a customized care plan tailored to your dog's individual needs and preferences.

Making Decisions About Euthanasia:

One of the most difficult decisions a pet owner may face is whether to euthanize their beloved companion. Euthanasia is a humane and compassionate option for ending your dog's suffering when their quality of life has significantly declined, and medical interventions are no longer effective or feasible. It's essential to consult with your veterinarian to discuss your dog's prognosis, treatment options, and quality of life considerations to make an informed decision about euthanasia. Trust your instincts and prioritize your dog's well-being and comfort above all else.

Coping with Grief and Loss:

Saying goodbye to a loved pet is an emotionally challenging experience that can evoke feelings of profound loss. It's essential to allow yourself to grieve and process your emotions in your own time and way. Seek support from friends, family, or pet loss support groups who understand and empathize with your pain. Memorialize your dog's life and legacy in meaningful ways, such as creating a photo album or formal portrait, planting a memorial garden, or making a donation to a pet charity in their honor. Remember that it's okay to seek professional help from a therapist or counselor if you're struggling to cope with your grief.

While facing the end of your dog's life is undoubtedly heartbreaking, it's also an opportunity to cherish the precious moments you've shared and honor the bond you've formed. By recognizing signs of declining health, you can make sure your companion's final days are filled with love, dignity, and comfort. Embrace the support of loved ones and take solace in the memories you've created together. Although your dog may no longer be physically present, its spirit will continue to live on in your heart.

12

Conclusion

As we reach the end of this journey through the world of dog ownership, I hope you've found the information in this book to be helpful and insightful. Just like any journey, embarking on the adventure of becoming a dog owner is filled with twists and turns, challenges and joys, but ultimately, it's a rewarding experience that enriches our lives in countless ways.

Throughout this book, we've covered everything from determining if you're ready for responsible dog ownership to selecting the right breed for your family, preparing your home and yard, ensuring your dog's nutrition and health, training and socialization tips, traveling with your canine companion, and even navigating end-of-life considerations with grace and compassion.

As you continue on your journey as a dog owner, remember that each day is an opportunity to learn and grow alongside your cherished friend. Hold dear the moments you share, embrace the challenges as opportunities for growth, and always look out for your dog's well-being and happiness.

Thank you for joining me on this journey, and may you and your canine companion enjoy a lifetime of love, laughter, and unforgettable memories.

    If you've found this book to be helpful in your journey as a first-time dog owner, I would greatly appreciate it if you could take a moment to leave a positive review on Amazon. Your feedback not only helps other readers discover this book but also encourages me to continue creating valuable resources for dog owners like you.

Blessings, Don Livingston

13

References

merican Kennel Club (AKC) - Website providing information on dog breeds, training, health, and care.

- Website: https://www.akc.org/

Association of American Feed Control Officials (AAFCO) - Organization setting standards for pet food nutrition.

- Website: https://www.aafco.org/

American Veterinary Medical Association (AVMA) - Resource for pet health information and veterinary care.

- Website: https://www.avma.org/

Pet Nutrition Alliance - Provides educational resources and guidelines on pet nutrition.

- Website: https://www.petnutritionalliance.org/

REFERENCES

American College of Veterinary Nutrition (ACVN) - Offers information on pet nutrition and dietary guidelines.

- Website: https://www.acvn.org/

Association for Pet Obesity Prevention - Provides resources and tools for managing pet weight and nutrition.

- Website: https://petobesityprevention.org/

Pet Care Services Association (PCSA) - Organization accrediting pet boarding and kennel facilities.

- Website: https://www.petcareservices.org/

About the Author

I grew up in the Pacific Northwest where much of life is lived outdoors, and frequent association with animals is common. On our small farm, nestled in the foothills of the Cascade Mountains, I had my first experience with dogs. It was here that I began a lifetime appreciation for these wonderful companions.

I have filled many roles in my life, including landscaper, educator, coach, pastor, writer. truck driver, carpenter, and more. I am also a husband, father, and grandfather. And it is my hope that I will also be known as a friend of dogs.

Don Livingston

Made in the USA
Las Vegas, NV
17 October 2024

97036232R00030